THE EXISTING MARKET TRAP

The Existing Market Trap

A PRIMER

Escaping the 13 Deadly Sins that Destroy Companies, Careers, and Portfolios

Al Ramadan
Christopher Lochhead
Jason Wellcome
Mary Grice

The Existing Market Trap. Copyright © 2025 by Alan Ramadan and Christopher Lochhead. All rights reserved. Printed in the United States of America. No part of this book may be used or reproduced in any manner whatsoever without written permission except in the case of brief quotations embodied in critical articles and reviews. For information, contact the publishers: Category Pirates.

Primer Edition

Edited by Chris Stanley and Brian Prugh
Front cover by Carrie Drew
Interior layout by Zoe Norvell

Library of Congress Cataloging-in-Publication Data has been applied for.

ISBN: 978-1-956934-75-5

AL:
To my mother, Lilian.
A constant source of inspiration, love, and life.
See you soaring in the Sierras.

CHRISTOPHER:
To my mum & dad Jackie (Leeke) Lochhead & Bruce Lochhead.

JASON:
To my daughter, Zoe.
May you always dance to your own rhythm and make the world listen.

MARY:
To my greatest joy ~ Finn, Fox & Quinn

Contents

Foreword	1
Introduction: The Trap We All Missed	5

Part I: Escaping The Existing Market Trap

1. Escaping the Existing Market Trap	13
2. The 13 Deadly Sins and When They Show Up	35
3. The Engineer's Dilemma	43
4. The Horizontal Tool Illusion	53
5. Existential Decline	63

Part II: What It Means (and Why It Matters)

6. What Escaping the Existing Market Trap Means for Your Company	73
7. What Escaping the Existing Market Trap Means for Your Career	79
8. What the Existing Market Trap Means for Your Portfolio	85
9. A Cautionary Tale: AI & Categories	91
Appendix A: For the Founders Who Took the Shot	101
Appendix B: The 13 Deadly Sins Taxonomy	104
Appendix C: This Is Where The Real Work Begins	107
Appendix D: Positioning	112
Appendix E: Capital Source, Methodology, and References	118
About the Authors	121

Foreword

From Authors and Partners of
Play Bigger

As we started working on our new book, *The Existing Market Trap*, something became clear:

Founders need this thinking NOW.

Like, right freaking now, because Artificial Intelligence (AI) is redrawing the map in real time—redesigning existing categories and creating opportunities for new categories at a rate never seen. This is forcing founders to explain what they are, why they matter, and how they will win in a world where AI is foundational.

They need language to describe what they are feeling.
They need a pattern to reveal what is holding them back.
And they need to know they are not crazy—and they are not alone.

So we decided to publish this primer edition—an early release of the frameworks and ideas we believe will help companies, careers, and portfolios escape the trap before it's too late.

We wrote it for founders, CEOs, executive teams, and investors building companies in real time. And here's what we've heard from you:

> You want the highlights first.
> And you want them fast.

That's why this primer edition is sharp, tight, and to the point.

It's not a storybook. It's a strategic field guide.

Inside, you'll find:
- What the Existing Market Trap is
- The 13 Deadly Sins that destroy companies, careers, and portfolios
- A few Deadly Sin chapters we believe every founder should read right now
- And why it matters for your company, your career, and your portfolio

It's designed to give you a complete framework—the high-leverage ideas, the diagnostic patterns, the early-stage escape plans.

The final edition of the book will go deeper:

More founder stories and Deadly Sin chapters (ten more).
More insights into what it means for your career.
More moments from inside the room.
More examples of how great companies escaped the Existing Market Trap—or didn't.
More detail on Category Design and what we've learned since our first book, *Play Bigger*.

For now, we want to get this primer edition into your hands while you're still in flight.

The final book will be the full debrief.

This is the first strike.

With love, sharp elbows, and absolute belief in you—

Al, Christopher, Jason & Mary

XOXOXOXO

Introduction

The Trap We All Missed

In 2016, we wrote a book called *Play Bigger: How Pirates, Dreamers, and Innovators Create and Dominate Markets*. It introduced the world to a new business discipline called Category Design—a way for companies and careers to break out of the pack and become Category Kings.

We showed how Category Kings don't just build great products—they design the space they live in and build belief in it. And when you do that, you don't have to compete on features or price. You become the only.

Our research—later published in Harvard Business Review—proved the point: Category Kings earn 76% of the market cap in their category. Not 30%. Not 51%. Seventy-six percent.

Since publishing *Play Bigger*, we've worked with more than 125 companies, helping them create new categories, shape markets, and build movements. Some went public. Some got acquired. Some became verbs.

Not all of them won—but the ones who did? They didn't out-feature their competitors. They changed the game.

But here's the part that's been bothering us for almost a decade:

We never clearly explained what Category Design is solving for. We laid out the solution in *Play Bigger*. But we skipped the first step, the most important step.

We never named the problem!

The guys who preach "Frame it, Name it, Claim it"

Didn't **Name** it.

Until now.

The Invisible Enemy

Every great innovation starts with defining the problem.

What problem are you solving and who are you solving it for?

It's a simple rule. But even the ones who preach it can forget to follow it.

We've never met a founder, entrepreneur, creator, pirate, dreamer, or innovator who wasn't passionate about their idea.

Often, that passion makes you hyper-focused on the solution.

It got us too.

This book is our correction.

It's the prequel to *Play Bigger*.

It names the problem Category Design solves:

> The Existing Market Trap.

What the Trap Looks Like

The Existing Market Trap is what you fall into when you build something new and compare it to something old.

You create a breakthrough product—and the world compares it to companies you don't even compete with, in categories you don't even belong in.

You launch something that could change the game and the analysts say, "Cool feature."

You raise money to build a movement, and get told to go chase a Total Addressable Market (TAM) slide.

It's what happens when you don't change the way people think about their problems—and the existing market defines what you are.

> From the very start, you're playing a competition game.
> From the very start, you're playing a market share game.
> From the very start, you're shoving your new thing into an old aisle.

And once you're trapped, everything gets harder:

> You burn cash without building belief
> You fight uphill for attention, leads, and relevance
> Your best people leave—because they want to work on something that matters

The Real Problem

Let's be crystal clear:

The Existing Market Trap isn't a marketing problem.
It's not a messaging problem.
It's not a product problem.

It's a problem identification problem.
A framing problem.
A belief problem.

And until you solve that, nothing else works the way it should.

The Path Forward

This primer names the problem.

And then it shows you how to beat it.

We've identified 13 Deadly Sins—patterns we've seen again and again in companies that fall into the trap.

Each one is a red flag.
A strategic blind spot.
A reason why otherwise great companies stall, shrink, or slowly lose their edge.

This primer is a field guide to escape.

It will help you see the trap you're in or avoid it entirely.
It will show you how to shift from competing to creating.
From explaining what you do … to owning what you are.

From being one of many ... to being the only.

Because once you see the Existing Market Trap, you can name it.
Once you name it, you can escape it.
And once you escape it, you can **Play Bigger**.

XOXOXOXO

Al, Christopher, Jason & Mary

P.S. As much as we blew it, we never did (or have) stopped thinking about the problem that category design solves. That obsession with the problem led to what comes next.

Part I

Escaping the Existing Market Trap

Escaping the Existing Market Trap

The Allure of An Existing Market Is The Most Seductive—And Expensive— Mistake In Business

Most companies don't fail because they build bad products. They fail because they get pulled into a market they didn't design—playing by rules they didn't set, in a game that was rigged. Before they ever showed up.

And the founders?
They didn't make a reckless error.
They followed the playbook.

There's proven demand.
There's a giant TAM.
There are companies making billions.

"We'll just take our slice," they say.

And since their product is clearly faster, cheaper, smarter, and just plain better—they assume the market will reward them.

That's the trap.

> They didn't define the category—they're trying to win inside someone else's.
> They didn't frame the problem—they're assuming the market already understands it.
> They didn't name the game—they're still playing the old one.

This is the **Existing Market Trap**.

It Sounds Smart—Until It's Not

The Existing Market Trap seduces founders, execs, and investors with all the signs of a smart strategy:

→ Jump into an established market
→ Solve a known problem
→ With a better product
→ A better brand
→ Target existing budgets
→ Get to 'product-market fit' faster

But what looks like a shortcut is a sinkhole.

Because here's the truth:

> The Category King earns 76% of the market cap.
> The market favors the incumbent.
> The game wasn't built for you—it was built by them.

> And everything—analyst comparisons, investor benchmarks, customer expectations—reinforces the leader, not the new entrant.

You're not just fighting a product.
You're fighting the frame.
The status quo.
And you're fighting human belief systems.

Because in the mind of the customer, the company that owns the problem becomes the solution.

The Real Costs of the Existing Market Trap

Let's start with the economic cost.

Grab a tasty beverage ... Let's talk numbers.
Over the past decade, ~$17 trillion[1] has been invested globally in startups, scaleups, and innovation—across venture capital, private equity, corporate venture arms, angels, seed funds, family offices, sovereign wealth funds, and accelerators.

And what do we have to show for it?

> An estimated 180,000 companies received funding
> 90% of them failed to deliver a return

Let that soak in.

A significant portion of that $13 trillion has likely vaporized.

---

1   For a detailed breakdown of capital sources, methodology, and references, see Appendix E.

In 2024 alone, over $2 trillion was lost due to failed bets.

And here's what we believe:

> $13 trillion in innovation didn't fail because the products were bad.
> It failed because the world never understood what the hell they were.

They let themselves be defined by the old category.
They never escaped the Existing Market Trap.

The Consequences Run Deep

The Existing Market Trap doesn't just destroy money.
It leaves wreckage across the entire innovation ecosystem.

Founder Burnout

> You build something extraordinary—but no one gets it.
> You rework the deck. Reposition. Pivot. Rebrand.
> Nothing sticks. Eventually, you start wondering if you're the problem.
> That's how smart, capable founders burn out.

Team Misalignment

> If there's no clear category, nobody knows what they're building toward.
> Fighting for market share isn't a mission. It's a morale crusher.
> Marketing pulls one way. Sales tells a different story.
> Product tries to please everyone. Top talent leaves.
> Culture erodes.

Strategic Drift

> You pinball between customer segments and use cases.
> There's no roadmap—just survival.
> You're chasing competition and not setting vision.
> Wandering around looking for money is not a strategy.

Go To Market (GTM) Confusion

> Sales can't explain what you do, so they make it up.
> Marketing defaults to feature dumps and branding arts and crafts.
> Analysts don't know where to slot you.
> You become a "nice to have," not a must-have.

Margin Pressure and Stalled Growth

> You hit a ceiling. Revenue plateaus. Customer Acquisition Cost (CAC) climbs.
> Pricing erodes. You start discounting.
> You're playing the game you swore you'd never play.

Missed Timing

> You miss the Initial Public Offering (IPO) window.
> You miss the category explosion.
> You either raise too early or go public too late.
> Either way—you leave beaucoup Benjamins on the table.

Undervalued Acquisitions

> When it's finally time to sell, you don't get acquired for your vision.
> You get picked up for parts. The acquirer gets the value.
> You become a slide in their deck.

Innovation Dies in the Shadows

> And maybe this is the worst one.
> Brilliant ideas, powerful technologies,
> world-changing potential—
> crushed not by failure of execution, but by failure of framing.

The Existing Market Trap doesn't just hurt your business.
It prevents the future from showing up.

Why Smart Founders Still Fall for It

Because everything about the Existing Market Trap feels rational.
There's a TAM slide.
There's a line item in customer budgets.
There's existing analyst coverage.
There's a Request for Proposal (RFP) on the street.

We're brainwashed to compete.

And in a world obsessed with speed to product-market fit, it's tempting to slide into something that already exists. Fit your product. Into an existing market.

But here's the truth:

The most dangerous place to build something new ... is inside something old.

The 13 Deadly Sins

Over the past 15 years, we've seen the same strategic breakdowns again and again.

We call them the 13 Deadly Sins of the Existing Market Trap.

They're not flukes. They're not founder flaws.
They're predictable failure patterns that show up in companies of every size, stage, and sector:

#1   The Engineer's Dilemma
#2   The Obviously Better Fallacy
#3   The Pinball Effect
#4   The Horizontal Tool Illusion
#5   The Product-Led Growth Myth
#6   The Market Share Fantasy
#7   The Sales Hype Machine
#8   The Distribution Delusion
#9   The VC Pressure Cooker
#10 The Conglomerate Identity Crisis
#11 The Brand Vanity Obsession
#12 The Point Tool Ceiling
#13 The Existential Decline

Most companies are committing one of these sins.
Some are committing multiple at the same time.

We'll go deep on a few of these sins in this primer—and share the rest in our final edition of *The Existing Market Trap* book and through *Deadly Sin Drops* along the way. The full EMT taxonomy is included in appendix B.

Markets Are People.
Categories Are Beliefs.

A market is a group of people—consumers or enterprises—who share a problem.

A category is the type of solution people believe can solve it.

It's the aisle in the grocery store.
Not the brand. Not the product.
The aisle.

Every aisle started with someone naming a problem no one even knew they had:

> You thought cities with stubby buildings were fine—until the elevator made skyscrapers.
> You thought your 3PM crash was normal—until energy shots hit the checkout line.
> You thought canned vegetables were fine—until the frozen food aisle showed up.
> You thought hailing taxis was fine—until rideshare made it feel ridiculous.

These founders evangelized a problem and built belief in a new category.

And here's what they didn't do:
They didn't build their way out of the trap with more features.

They sharpened the problem.
They clarified the solution.
They declared the category.
They made the market believe in something new.

Belief is the most powerful product you can ship.
And most companies never ship it.

The Journey of Category Design and Market Creation

> The way out of the Existing Market Trap isn't building more features.
> It's building more belief.

Belief that the problem matters.
Belief that your solution is the right answer.
Belief that you are the leader of a new category of solutions.

Belief doesn't happen by accident.
It happens by design.

Category Design is the discipline of building belief—internally, externally, and repeatedly—until the market sees your company as the obvious leader of a category only you can own.

It builds across four distinct phases.
Each phase pulls more people into orbit.
Each one turns belief into momentum.
And momentum into gravity.

Let's walk through what that journey looks like—starting with the hardest part: finding the truth.

PHASE 1.
Market Creation Strategy – Find the Truth

This is where the escape begins.

Where Are You At?
Category + Existing Market Trap Assessment

Start by getting brutally honest.

Let's start with the facts and where you really are.

First, assess the category opportunity by interviewing founders, execs, customers, partners, and investors to identify:
- The problem you solve
- Who has it
- What it's costing them
- What they're doing about it (and why it's not working)

Second, diagnose the Existing Market Trap you're already in—or barreling toward—by:
- Running the EMT diagnostic to see what sins you might be committing
- Mapping external signals: analyst language, competitor framing, market noise
- Spotting the traps that could shrink or misframe your value

This isn't about your product.

It's about the problem—the consequences of not solving it and the massive rewards of getting it right.

It's about understanding where you are trapped or have the potential to be trapped.

Where Could We Go: The Journey to a Market Thesis

Before you can write a Point of View (POV), you have to understand what it's really about.

This phase is messy. It's not a checklist—it's a search.

You're in the fog.
You're debating the problem, the name, the audience.
You're hearing twelve different versions of what you are.
You're not sure what is signal and what is noise.

But this is the work of this phase and it's how belief begins to take shape.

Your job is to listen for the strongest reactions and sharpest signals.
The edges. The "*I love that.*" The "*I hate that.*"
The minus 1. The plus 1. Don't be afraid of negatives, they are just as powerful as positives.
The stuff that makes the room go silent.
That's your wayfinding system.

And what you're searching for is this:
- What's the real problem in the world?
- Who is feeling it first—and who's next?
- What happens if it goes unsolved?
- What does success look like for our customer?
- What kind of solution is needed?
- What kind of market would form around it?

You don't invent the category, you uncover it—through decisions, tension, and debate.
The answer is already in the room. You just have to stand it up.

And when belief finally clicks, the Blueprint starts to emerge.

You're not just exploring a market.
You're discovering the one your company was meant to lead.

Create your POV (Source Code)
Out of the mist, alignment begins to form.

A first cut is shared.
More discussion, more pushback, maybe even some pie-throwing.
This is a time for real dialogue—jamming, dreaming, fighting for clarity.

POVs Frame it (the problem), Name it (the villain), and Claim it (the category).

They use some, or all, of these ten elements to create a powerful POV:
1. Frame the Problem
2. Describe the Problem
3. Name the Villain
4. Quantify the Ramifications
5. Explain that It Doesn't Have to Be This Way
6. Share a Vision for the Future
7. Introduce the New Category
8. Explain How It Works (Blueprint)
9. Reveal the Outcomes
10. Issue a Call to Action

This becomes your source code, everything else flows from here.

And executive alignment? It's not a moment—it's a rhythm.

PHASE 2.
Mobilization – Make It Real Inside

Category Design only works when the CEO and exec team are all in. And it also demands real focus from the whole company.

Once the POV is locked, the company must now become it.

This is the internal activation phase—when belief turns into behavior.

Commitment Ceremony

This is the symbolic and strategic moment where everything shifts. The CEO stands in front of the company and says, "This is where we're going." We sometimes call it the "Burning of the Boats."

This isn't a campaign, this is the new operating system. It's how you stop being what you were—and start becoming what you must be.

Create the Essentials

Start by translating your POV into the Essentials—the critical documents and assets that embed belief across every team:

- All-Hands Deck
- Keynote Presentation
- Sales / Corporate Deck
- Message Framework
- Analyst Briefing
- Investor Deck
- Category Blueprint Visual

This is the minimum set to make the POV real, it must be internal, external, visible—and repeated.

Stand Up Your Category Operating Model

As you refine the Essentials, something bigger starts to take shape.

What starts as a POV becomes a strategic system—one that transforms how you build, communicate, sell, hire, raise, and scale.

In category-led companies, the POV isn't owned by marketing. It's embedded in the operating system of the company.

We call this the Category Operating Model and it's how belief becomes behavior—how strategy becomes muscle memory across the entire business.

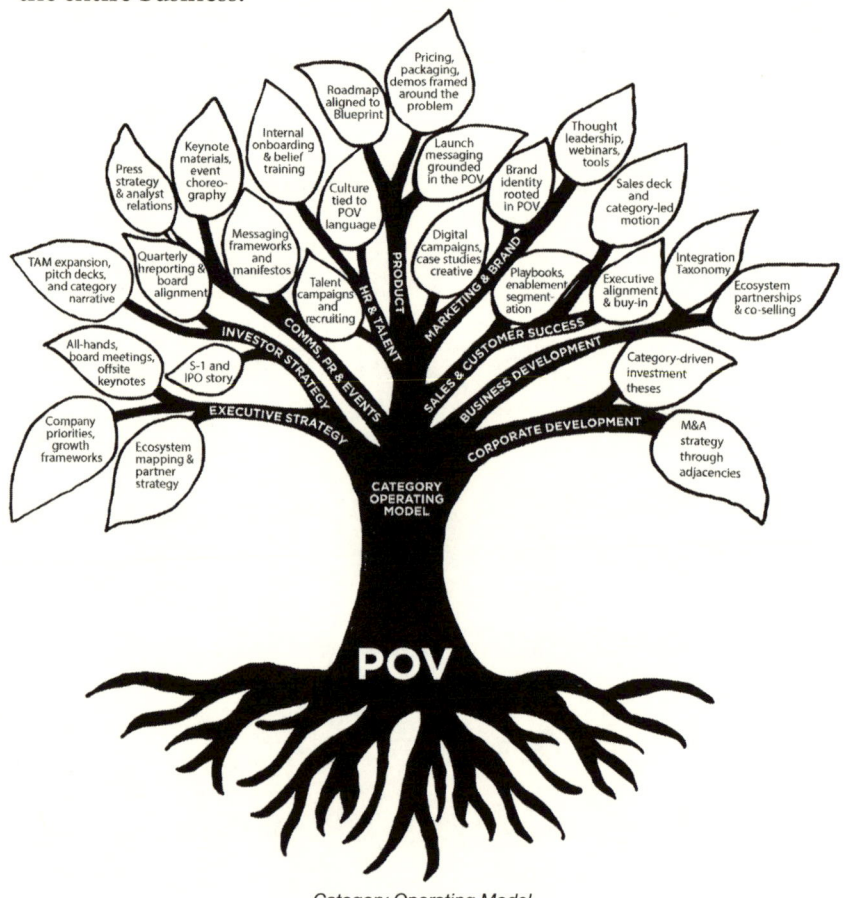

Category Operating Model

Think of it like this:

> The POV is the root system.
> The Category Operating Model is the trunk.
> Belief spreads through every branch of the company.
> Core artifacts are the leaves.

Some companies write a POV and stop.
Category leaders build an operating model around it.

That's the difference between a deck and a movement.
Between a message and a moat.

Build a Lightning Strike Plan

This is where you plan the moment the world hears your POV.

Key questions:
- Who's the audience?
- Where do they congregate?
- Do we host or hijack?
- What do we want them to believe? (Hint: It's the POV)
- What assets need to exist?
- Who needs to be trained and ready?

Pick a date and venue where your target audience will be congregating and build a work back plan. It needs to be detailed and you should appoint a strike leader to drive the process.

PHASE 3.
Lightning Strike Execution – Make It Real Outside

Your first Lightning Strike is the moment belief moves outside the building.

The world is about to see what only your team has believed until now.

This isn't a product launch, it's a category launch, a public declaration that the game has changed—and you're leading the new one.

A Lightning Strike Is a Strategic Shockwave.

It's engineered to:

> Change how the market thinks
> Frame the problem in a new way
> Name the category
> Recast your company as the obvious leader
> Force competitors, customers, and analysts to react

It's not just visibility. It's building belief in a new market.

The Core Ingredients of a Lightning Strike

To hit hard, a Strike must synchronize message, moment, and motion across the company.

Core Activities:

- CEO as evangelist – public narrative + bold declaration
- Analyst + media briefings – validate the problem + lock in external framing
- Customer proof – stories that validate the belief
- Product, brand, and sales go live in sync – POV in every motion
- Flagship campaign or event – your big bang moment

- Top of funnel ignites – new energy, new leads, new language
- Early adopters engage – and help spread the belief

The best Strikes feel like a sudden, unexpected surge of energy in the market—because they are.

Focus the Strike

You don't need to launch it to everyone at once. The most effective Strikes are precise, targeting a node in the market where belief can spread fast:

- Geographic – e.g., Asia Pacific launch with regional evangelists
- Vertical – e.g., claim leadership in Healthcare, Fintech, Manufacturing
- Functional – e.g., win the CFO, CMO, Head of Procurement
- Personal/Identity-driven – e.g., empower creators, builders, operators

Focus amplifies force. Strike where it matters most—then widen the orbit.

Strike Feedback Loops

Every Lightning Strike creates energy.
And it creates reactions.
And more signals.

Capture them, they are your external beacons.

Use them to sharpen your POV, refine your Blueprint, evolve your sales motion and feed belief back inside the company.

This is how Lightning Strikes power the flywheel of belief.

Each one makes the next stronger.

PHASE 4.
Strike Ops – Repeat, Refine, Dominate

Many companies stop after the first strike.
Category Kings never do.

This is where belief compounds—again and again.

Strike Ops is a multi-year, cross-functional system of market conditioning. It's not a campaign calendar; it's the ongoing orchestration of belief.

The best companies run two Lightning Strikes per year. Each one creates a surge of momentum—and then feeds new energy back into the system.

The Belief Flywheel
Every Strike:
- Adds new believers
- Introduces new research
- Adds proof points
- Launches new products
- Expands the Blueprint
- Brings on new customers
- Attracts new hires
- Grows the ecosystem
- Trains the market
- Widens the gap

The POV gets sharper.
The belief gets stronger.
The distance between leader and followers gets bigger.

This Is the Self-Fulfilling Prophecy of Category Leadership

The beautiful thing is each Lightning Strike becomes a forcing function across the company:

- Product teams fight to demo their new product during the keynote
- Sales leaders campaign to get their customer on stage
- Marketing pushes reach, narrative, and creative
- Investors show up
- Analysts adopt your language
- Competitors start copying your POV
- Partners want in
- The market says, *"They're the leader."*

That's not magic, that's Category Design—at scale.

This is how belief loops, lifts, and locks in.

This is how you escape the Existing Market Trap—Not for a quarter, but forever.

Wrapping Up: Escaping the Existing Market Trap

The Existing Market Trap isn't a fluke.
It's not a one-time mistake.

It's a pattern—baked into the startup ecosystem, reinforced by consensus capital, and hiding inside every TAM slide, category label, and "go-to-market" plan.

It convinces great founders to play small.
It turns game-changing ideas into misunderstood features.

It pushes visionary teams into categories they didn't create and can't win.

And it's everywhere.

We believe the Existing Market Trap is the single greatest destroyer of innovation, growth, and founder potential in the market today.

The good news? You can escape.

The companies that break free don't just reposition in an existing market. They build belief in a new one using Category Design.

It's not branding. It's not messaging. It's not positioning (see appendix D).

It's a complete rethinking of what your company is, what problem it solves, and what kind of future it's here to build.

It's how companies like Qualtrics, Docusign, Apple and many others didn't just win … they changed the rules.

> We've shown you the trap.
> We've shown you the cost.
> And now we've shown you the way out.

What Comes Next

In the chapters that follow, we'll go deep into how the Existing Market Trap actually shows up—through the 13 Deadly Sins.

These are the real-world failure patterns that pull teams off track, stall growth, and cause great companies to get stuck.

We'll take you inside three critical ones:
- The Engineer's Dilemma: when you lead with brilliant tech, but the market doesn't feel the pain
- The Horizontal Tool Illusion: when you're useful to everyone, but strategic to no one
- Existential Decline: when you built the category ... but forgot to evolve it

We'll show you what they look like.
We'll tell stories of companies that escaped—and what changed when they did.

We'll also go deeper on the transformation that happens when a company breaks free from the trap and starts building the market instead of chasing one.

You'll see what this shift means not just for your strategy, but for your company culture, your leadership/career and your portfolio.

And finally, we'll close with a cautionary tale—one you might be living through right now—about what happens when companies try to bolt AI onto the end of an outdated story.

This isn't a book about how to position your product in an existing market.

It's about how to design the market you were meant to lead and build belief in a new solution.

Hey ho, let's go.

The 13 Deadly Sins and When They Show Up

How The Existing Market Trap Unfolds Across The Category Lifecycle

Not all sins show up at the same time.

In the last chapter, we introduced the 13 Deadly Sins—patterns that sabotage great companies, careers, and portfolios when they fall into the Existing Market Trap.

But here's what we've learned:

WHEN a sin shows up is just as important as WHAT the sin is.

Because most companies aren't making obviously bad decisions.

They're doing what seems reasonable for where they are in their growth strategy. They're following advice. They're moving fast. They're doing what worked before.

But when you zoom out and look across company evolution and the category lifecycle, you start to see a pattern:

The Deadly Sins cluster.

They emerge at key inflection points—when executives are defining, scaling, or defending their category—and if you don't recognize the sins early, they compound fast.

The Category Lifecycle

As we explained in *Play Bigger*, every great category follows a predictable arc.

Whether you're building enterprise software, a consumer app, or a radically new model for your industry—categories are living systems.

And like all systems, they evolve.

This is the Category Lifecycle.

Knowing where you are in it can be the difference between leading a movement ... or getting left behind.

Define Phase: The Battle for Belief
This is where it begins.

> The problem hasn't been named

> The villain hasn't been identified
> The category doesn't exist

This is the market chaos phase. The market doesn't "get it" yet—and that's the point.
Your job is to teach them. To frame the pain so sharply they can't unsee it.

Most sins in this phase are related to Strategic Invisibility—not being seen for what you really are or being buried deep down in an enterprise.

Develop Phase: The Fight to Become Category King
Now the battle is on.

> The problem is understood
> The category is emerging
> You're no longer alone—but you want to win

This is the battleground for dominance—and it's where the Category Contenders emerge. Explore the data and patterns behind these breakout companies in our Category Contenders[2]

But as pressure mounts, sins begin to surface—especially when growth outruns clarity.

This is where companies mistakenly scale confusion instead of conviction.

---

2 research at https://www.PlayBigger.com/en-us/CategoryContenders/.

Dominate Phase: The Risk of Decline

You won.

> You built the aisle
> You're the default
> You're the name people know

But now ... the urgency is gone.
The problem you solved feels "done."
And the market has moved on—but you haven't.

This is where Category Kings fade—not because of product failure, but because of category stagnation.

Mapping the Sins to the Lifecycle

Here's where the sins often show up:

Strategically Invisible (Define)
The market doesn't understand what you really are.
These sins make you invisible before you even get started:

#1 The Engineer's Dilemma – Leading with technology instead of pain

#2 The Obviously Better Fallacy – Feature comparisons instead of framing a new game

#3 The Pinball Effect – Inconsistent story, scattered perception

#4 The Horizontal Tool Illusion – Useful to everyone, essential to no one

#5 The Product-Led Growth Myth – Expecting usage to build belief

Growth Is Breaking You (Develop)

You're scaling—but the strategy isn't keeping up.
These sins show up when velocity outruns vision:

#6   The Market Share Fantasy – Trying to win a piece of someone else's category
#7   The Sales Hype Machine – Pushing features instead of selling a future
#8   The Distribution Delusion – Big reach, little resonance
#9   The VC Pressure Cooker – Growth goals with no category clarity

You're Losing the Plot (Dominate)

You built the category—but didn't evolve it.
These sins show how great companies become legacy:

#10   The Conglomerate Identity Crisis – Too many products, no unifying story
#11   The Brand Vanity Obsession – Internal story ≠ external belief
#12   The Point Tool Ceiling – Solving part of the problem, getting sidelined
#13   Existential Decline – Still the leader—in a category no one cares about any longer

A Note on Timing

Just because a sin usually shows up in one phase doesn't mean it can't appear earlier—or later.

Some sins are recurring.
Some evolve into new forms.
Some show up quietly, then explode.

But knowing when they tend to emerge gives you power.

It gives you a diagnostic lens.
It helps you anticipate, identify, and escape before the damage is done.

What's Next

In the next chapters, we'll go deep into three of the common Deadly Sins:
- The Engineer's Dilemma
- The Horizontal Tool Illusion
- Existential Decline

Let's get into it.

THE ENGINEER'S DILEMMA

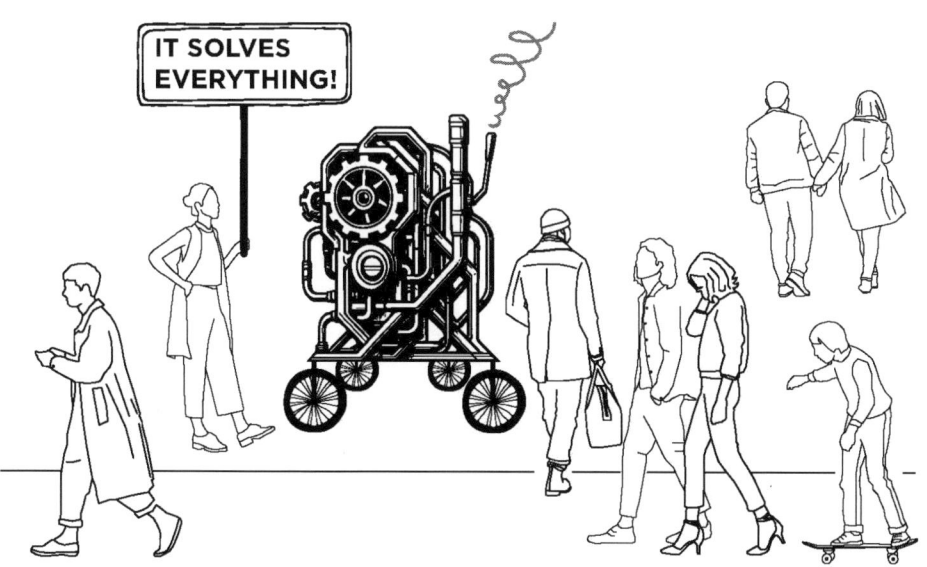

The Engineer's Dilemma

A Solution Looking For A Problem.

You've built something brilliant.
Technically elegant. Architecturally sound.
Your team is proud. The demo is slick. The use cases are endless.

And yet ... no one cares.

> You're not failing.
> You're just invisible.

You're leading with the solution instead of the problem.
You're building features instead of belief.

The market doesn't reward elegance.
It rewards urgency.

And urgency starts with belief.

Key Signal

> You're pitching to users, not decision-makers.
> Prospects say "cool tech"—but don't act.
> Investors ask for a simpler story.
> Your sales team keeps asking for "a better way to explain it."
> People treat you like a vitamin, not an aspirin.

What It Means

> You're assuming great tech wins market share.
> But in a noisy world, new features don't sell—new problems do.

What's Really Going Wrong

> You're overly focused on the product.
> You're not anchoring it in a problem the market can feel.
> You haven't built belief.

Without a Point of View, even the best tech gets dropped into the wrong bucket—or ignored entirely.

The Escape

> Start with the pain.
> Frame the problem so clearly that the solution becomes obvious—and inevitable.
> Name the villain.

Don't just build something amazing.
Build the story that makes it matter.

ClearMetal: The Company That Escaped—Twice

Three Stanford founders. One garage.
A bold idea at the intersection of machine learning and global trade.

ClearMetal (originally called Tilikin) set out to predict where freight was and when it would arrive.

They had the talent. The funding. A technically sophisticated platform. But no one knew what to call them.

"Are you a visibility tool?"
"Like Flexport?"
"A dashboard for logistics?"

They weren't.
But they hadn't yet built the belief to say what they really were.

Naming the Problem

When we started working with ClearMetal, the product was real. But the category wasn't.

They were using advanced Machine Learning (ML) to predict shipment arrivals, identify bottlenecks, and re-optimize supply flows. But no one could feel the pain.

After weeks of field interviews, a new pattern emerged:

> Global commerce had changed.
> Amazon had reset expectations.
> "On time" now meant "real time."

The problem?

Shipping infrastructure hadn't kept up.
The systems couldn't tell you what happened today—let alone predict tomorrow.

We named the villain: *The Now Economy Gap*.
And the problem: Outdated IT in the age of Amazon.

It wasn't just a logistics issue.
It was a systemic economic threat.

Defining the Category

With the problem and villain in place, we worked with the team to define the new category:
Predictive Logistics.

It wasn't about where a shipment was.
It was about where it would be—and what to do about it.

The POV was simple:

"You can't win in the Now Economy using yesterday's systems."

ClearMetal wasn't a control tower or a Business Intelligence (BI) tool. It was a learning platform for global freight.

And that distinction gave them gravity.

The Lightning Strike

We launched the category at a Lightning Strike in Long Beach—one of the busiest shipping hubs in the U.S.

The event brought together execs from ports, forwarders, carriers, and brands.

We walked through the Now Economy Gap and positioned Predictive Logistics as the solution.

> "Legacy logistics shows you what happened yesterday. Predictive Logistics tells you what happens tomorrow."

It landed.

The press picked it up.
Analysts wanted briefings.
And for the first time, strategic buyers understood what ClearMetal actually was.

Belief showed up.

The Pivot

A few years later, ClearMetal realized their best customers weren't carriers.
They were retailers. Like BIG ones.

Retailers didn't just want to track freight.
They wanted to manage customer expectations.

And that shifted everything.

The product didn't change—but the problem did.
The buyer changed.
So the category had to change, too.

Evolving the POV

In 2020, ClearMetal launched a new category:
Continuous Delivery Experience (CDX).
The new POV said:

> "Fulfillment is the new front line of customer experience."

Retailers didn't just want visibility—they wanted predictability. They wanted to know what was coming, when, and how it would impact promises made to customers.

CDX reframed logistics as an experience layer for modern brands.

And ClearMetal made the leap.

Outcome

In 2021, ClearMetal was acquired by Project44.

"What we gain from ClearMetal is a holistic platform," said Jason Duboe, Chief Growth Officer at project44. "They have large customers with advanced use cases ... we can now move upstream."

ClearMetal didn't just escape the Engineer's Dilemma.
They evolved their POV—twice.
And proved that great companies don't just build features.

They build **belief**.

The Escape Plan

Start with the pain – Lead with the problem, not the product.
Name the villain – Make the source of the pain visible.
Define the user – Design for someone, not everyone.
Design the category – Lead the new game, don't play the old one.
Light the fuse – Launch with force. Make the market feel it.

Play Bigger POV

You can't convert people who don't feel the pain.
Until you name the problem, you'll stay misunderstood.
Until you name the villain, you'll stay miscategorized.
Until you claim the category, you'll stay invisible.

Build belief first.

Then build everything else.

THE HORIZONTAL TOOL ILLUSION

4

The Horizontal Tool Illusion

When You're Useful To Everyone— And Strategic To No One

"Our product can do so many things ... but we're not getting credit for any of it."

It starts as a strength.
Your product is flexible. Broad. Adaptable.
Everyone can use it.

But no one believes they need it.

That's the danger of the Horizontal Tool Illusion.

You build a platform with wide applicability.
And the market responds ... with confusion.

You're not seen as strategic.
You're not positioned as essential.
You're admired—but not adopted.
You're compared to everything—and chosen for nothing.

You're not failing.
You're just strategically invisible at scale.

This is one of the deadliest sins in the Define phase—because it feels like traction, but it's actually an illusion.

What It Feels Like

> Usage across functions—but no clear buyer
> Customers say, "we love it"—but your deal size is small
> You're winning logos, but not belief
> Every sales conversation starts with, "So ... what do you guys actually do?"

You're in the aisle—but the shelf you're on doesn't match your value.

Why It Happens

> It happens when you prioritize product flexibility over problem clarity.
> You build something that can be used by anyone.
> But because it's not designed for someone, no one fights for it.

The market doesn't reward versatility.
It rewards specificity.

Broad utility might win attention.
But only clear problems create urgent demand.

Qualtrics: The Company That Escaped

When we first met CEO Ryan Smith and the Qualtrics team in Provo, they were already successful:

> A loyal user base
> A flexible product
> Strong revenue growth
> Unicorn status

But Ryan was frustrated:

"I keep getting called Survey Software on steroids."

It wasn't just inaccurate.
It was limiting.

Because deep down, Ryan knew what they were really building:
A system to help companies understand how people were experiencing their products, brands, and workplaces.

But no one could see it.

They were stuck in the Horizontal Tool Illusion.
Broad capability. Vague identity. No gravity.

The Bigger Problem
We started with a simple question:

"What do you actually get from a survey?"

Answer: insight into how someone feels—about a product, a service, a brand, a moment.

Human factors data—the feelings, expectations, and perceptions—was the real value.

We gave it a name: Experience Data (X Data).

And once we named it, everything shifted.

Ryan and his team realized:

"We're not measuring transactions. We're measuring experiences."

The real problem wasn't survey fatigue.
It was experience blindness—a massive misalignment between what companies thought they were delivering… and what people actually felt.

Naming the Villain
We called it: **The Experience Gap**.

To make it real, we backed it with data:

> 80% of CEOs believed they were delivering great experiences
> Only 8% of customers agreed

That 72-point delta became the villain.

Everyone felt it.
No one had named it—until now.

The Category
Once the Experience Gap was named, the solution became obvious.

To close the gap, companies needed a system to measure, understand, and act on X Data—across every part of the business.

We called it: **Experience Management**.
Shortened it to XM. And it stuck.

It wasn't a feature.
It was a new layer of enterprise infrastructure—on par with CRM, ERP, and HCM.

And Qualtrics became the company that delivered it.

Internal Mobilization

The turning point came in a founder-led exec meeting.

Ryan walked the team through the full POV:

> The villain: The Experience Gap
> The vision: Revolutionizing Experience
> The category: Experience Management
> The Blueprint: XM across the enterprise

Then he said:

"I'm about to make a very big strategic step—from surveys to XM.
"And I want you all with me."

One by one, every exec said yes.

That was the moment.
The Burning of the Boats.

From that day forward, Qualtrics wasn't a survey company.
They were XM.

Lightning Strike: Reframing the Market

The external Strike came at Qualtrics' annual Insights Conference.

3,000+ attendees.
And one huge shift.

Ryan stood on stage and reframed the problem:

"What you care about isn't the survey—it's what it measures.
"It's experience."

Then he dropped the stat:

"80% of CEOs think they're delivering great experiences.
"Only 8% of customers agree."

There was an audible groan.
Everyone in the room felt it.

Then came the platform:

The XM Platform
The Four core experiences of business:
    CX (Customer Experience)
    EX (Employee Experience)
    PX (Product Experience)
    BX (Brand Experience)

"These are the four corners of the modern enterprise."

The POV landed.
XM was real.
And the market moved.

Outcome

Qualtrics restructured around the XM Blueprint.

They stopped delivering survey tools—and started delivering systems.

> SAP acquired Qualtrics for $8 billion in 2018
> They went public in 2020 with a $27 billion market cap
> XM became their ticker symbol

Then came the next evolution.

In 2021, they realized that capturing X-data wasn't enough. To truly understand the experiences of their customers and employees, companies needed actionable insights from every channel. The kinds of insights they could get without ever asking a question, based on customer service chats, social media, product reviews. And Omnichannel XM was born.

More recently, as generative AI has made it possible to understand and respond to every customer, Qualtrics is leading into the next seismic shift in XM by building AI Experience Agents to understand *interactions*. And create experiences tuned for human connection, based on decades of Experience Management.

They went from being compared to SurveyMonkey—

To being recognized as the creators and Kings of Experience Management.

They built **belief**. In the problem. In the solution. And as the leader in the market.

The Escape Plan

Define the user – Don't be useful to everyone. Be essential to someone.

Frame the problem – Show what your solution reveals that no one else can see.

Make it strategic – Utility doesn't drive urgency. Systems do.

Own the aisle – Don't settle for being a top-right tool. Design the aisle you want to dominate.

Light the fuse – Mobilize the company. Launch with force. Make the category feel real.

Play Bigger POV

If you're useful to everyone, you're often valued by no one.

Horizontal tools don't win categories.
They win features—and then get commoditized.

Category Kings don't build tools.
They build strategic systems that solve urgent, high-value problems.

And they build belief that only they can lead the category that matters.

THE EXISTENTIAL DECLINE

5

The Existential Decline

When The Category You Created Stops Creating Demand

"We're still the leader. But the market's not listening anymore."

You built the category.
You named the problem.
You rallied the market.
You became the default choice.
You owned the aisle.

And then ... something shifted.

The problem you solved became expected.
The urgency faded.
What once sparked belief now feels like table stakes.
Competitors started bundling what you built—for free.

You're still winning deals.

But the category isn't growing.

And the energy that once drove momentum … is gone.

This is Existential Decline—the quiet drift into irrelevance that happens when the category you created stops creating demand.

Think Xerox. Kodak. HP. Evernote.

What It Feels Like

- You're still hitting numbers—but growth has slowed
- Your category is fully adopted—but no longer differentiated
- You're reacting to the market—not shaping it
- Your team is executing—but not inspired
- The press has moved on
- Competitors are repositioning around your gaps

Someone on your exec team asks:

"Are we still leading—or just maintaining?"

This is the danger of the Dominate phase of the Category Lifecycle.

You won.
But the problem you solved feels … done.

And the market is asking:

"What's next?"

You don't have a good answer.

Why It Happens

Category dominance is a gift—and a trap.

> You created belief.
> You scaled fast.
> You became the Category King.

But kings only stay kings if they evolve the game.

> You can't scale off a problem the market thinks is already solved.

The category becomes a box.
And the longer you stay in it, the harder it is to grow out of it.

Docusign: The Company That Escaped

Docusign was the undisputed king of eSignature.

They defined the category.
They were the verb—the ultimate signal of category domination.
They captured the lion's share of market cap, revenue, and mindshare.

But by 2020, eSignature had become commoditized.

Microsoft bundled it.
Adobe bundled it.
Startups offered it for free.
Customers saw it as a feature—not a strategy.

Internally, the Docusign team could feel it.
They were still winning.
But they weren't leading.

They had two choices:

Stay the kings of a declining category—
Or build belief in something bigger.

The Problem
Docusign realized the category wasn't broken.
It had just stopped expanding.

There were over 500 competitors doing some version of eSignature.

The real issue wasn't just signing.
It was everything before—and after—the signature.

Companies were spending billions managing contracts with disconnected tools:

- Redlining in Microsoft Word or Google Docs
- Negotiating via email
- Filing PDFs in cloud storage
- Manually tracking obligations post-signature

Agreements weren't dynamic.
They were fragmented.
They were a mess.

Naming the Villain
Docusign named the villain: **The Agreement Trap**.

A world where mission-critical agreements are locked inside static files, disconnected from the systems that run the business.

To make the problem undeniable, they commissioned a study with Deloitte.

The results:

> 92% of organizations struggle to extract data from agreements.
> 85% don't track post-signature obligations.
> Nearly $2 trillion in business value is lost or delayed every year due to agreement mismanagement.

This wasn't a process problem.
It was a board-level risk.

The villain had a number. And it was massive.

The Decision: Burn the Boats

In early 2024, Docusign made a decision.

They wouldn't just evolve their messaging.
They weren't going to do a Repositioning (they had already tried that).
They would expand their identity.

At a company-wide all-hands meeting, President of Growth, Robert Chatwani, led the Burning of the Boats Ceremony:

"This is the next chapter in our journey.
"And there's no going back."

The team laid out:

> The problem: Fragmentation and PDFs everywhere
> The villain: The Agreement Trap
> The new category: Intelligent Agreement Management (IAM)

This wasn't messaging.
It was a transformation.

And it was the moment belief moved to the entire organization.

The Lightning Strike

Docusign's category launch culminated at Momentum 2024, their flagship event in Manhattan.

CEO Allan Thygesen, President of Growth Robert Chatwani, and CPO Dmitri Krakovsky stood on stage and declared:

"We spent the last two decades changing how agreements are signed. "Now we're changing how they're managed."

They didn't launch features.
They launched a new category: Intelligent Agreement Management (IAM).

The keynote walked through:

> The scale of the Agreement Trap
> The vision for IAM
> Real-world use cases across sales, procurement, and legal
> The IAM platform: create, commit, manage
> Strategic integrations and data unlocks

The strike hit hard:

Analyst coverage surged.
The media reframed Docusign.
Strategic deal size grew.
And internally, the team aligned:

"We're not the eSignature company anymore."

Outcome

Investors responded.

A year after the strike, on their earnings call, CEO Allan Thygesen reported that 18% of revenue now comes from IAM.

The stock jumped 16%
Shares are up over 50% since the first Strike

Why?

Because investors know how rare it is for a company that defined the original category ... to define the next one.

Intel didn't create GPUs. NVIDIA did.
Google didn't define Generative AI. OpenAI did.
Docusign did it. Under the pressure of the public markets.

The Escape Plan

> Recognize the shift – If your category isn't creating demand, it's time to reframe.
> Reclaim urgency – Quantify the next problem. Make it impossible to ignore.
> Mobilize the team – This isn't messaging. It's transformation.
> Strike with force – Don't whisper a new story. Declare a new agenda for the market.
> Evolve before you're replaced – The market will move—with or without you.

Play Bigger POV

You can't dominate a category that's stopped creating demand.

Legendary companies don't just scale what they built.
They design what comes next.

They build belief again—at a higher level.

And they pull the market into orbit around a new problem, a new vision, and a new category.

Part II

What It Means
(And why it matters)

6

What Escaping the Existing Market Trap Means for Your Company

Clarity. Conviction. Category Power.

Escaping the Existing Market Trap isn't about fixing your messaging.
It's not about "tightening the pitch."
It's not a new website, a rebrand, or a repositioning exercise.

It's a strategic reset.
A new lens on business.
Because she who designs the category is best positioned to dominate it.

Escaping the Existing Market Trap means stepping out of the

game you've been shoved into—and designing the one where you are the only choice.

It means:

> Framing the problem so sharply the market can't unsee it
> Naming the villain so clearly that everything else looks broken
> Claiming the high ground with a Point of View that creates belief
> Launching Lightning Strikes that move the market to your advantage
> Aligning your team around a vision big enough to last a decade

Escaping the Existing Market Trap means you stop competing on features and benefits—and start creating the market categories of the future.

You Don't React to the Market—You Design It

Most people accept the market the way it is.
The same way they accept the weather.
It's an external thing. It happens to us.
We react when it does its thing.

This broken mental scaffolding is everywhere in business.

Open any business book, watch any CNBC segment, and you'll hear it:

> *"GM's revenue is down this quarter due to softness in demand."*
> *"NVIDIA beat Wall Street expectations as GPU demand surged."*

As if demand just happened to them.
As if it started raining TAM.

But markets aren't weather.

They don't just happen. People make them happen.

Our businesses are not a function of the market.

The market is a function of our business.
(Paraphrasing Michael E. Gerber, author of *The E-Myth*.)

The Proof

> Before Spanx, total global demand for shapewear was zero.
> Before OpenAI, global demand for generative AI was zero.
> Before Ford Motor Company, worldwide demand for automobiles was zero.
> Before Bookies Pizza, total Santa Cruz demand for inauthentic Detroit pizza was ... zero.

Markets don't preexist your success.

Markets are created by category designers who make people believe in a new possibility.

When You Design a New Category ...

> You don't get compared.
> You don't get commoditized.
> You don't get asked what category you're in—because you are the category.

The Shift

When you escape the Existing Market Trap:

> Customers feel urgency, not just curiosity.
> Investors buy into your vision, not just your metrics.
> Analysts write about you, not just "the space."
> Talent wants to join—because they believe in the mission.
> Your team aligns—because the story is simple, strong, and strategic

You go from pushing deals ...
To pulling the market toward you.

That's why we don't like the phrase "go-to-market." Why would you go to the market if you could make the market come to you?

You go from being "in a hot space" ...
To being the reason the space is hot.

The Real Outcome

Escaping the Existing Market Trap doesn't just mean you get seen.

It means you get understood, believed in, and backed—by everyone that matters.

It means you stop answering the question:

"What exactly is it that you do?"

And start hearing:

"We need what only you can deliver."

The Great Companies Don't Fit In

They don't chase market share.

They don't copy competitors.

They don't scale without a story.

They don't cling to a category that no longer creates demand.

They create the market.

They expand the category.

They define what comes next.

They create belief.

Escaping the Existing Market Trap means you stop letting the market define you—and you start designing it instead.

Let's build that legendary company.

What Escaping the Existing Market Trap Means for Your Career

*Stop Being Misunderstood.
Start Being Undeniable.*

There's a brutal truth we've learned after working with hundreds of founders, execs, and operators:

The Existing Market Trap doesn't just trap companies.
It traps careers.

We've seen brilliant product leaders get labeled as "builders," not strategists.
We've seen visionary CMOs miscast as "brand people" in companies that had no POV.
We've seen CEOs who could have been category creators reduced

to just another founder in just another crowded market.
We've seen amazing marketers who could be the next generation of category designers get wrapped around the obviously better re-positioning axle.

Not because they lacked skill.
Not because they lacked vision.
But because the market didn't understand what they were really doing.

Sound familiar?

You've done the work.
You've led the team.
You've pushed the product.
You've raised the money.

But somehow ...

You're not being seen for what you actually are.
The world sees your new vision through an old lens.

That's what the Existing Market Trap does.

And escaping it isn't just about your company's future.

It's about your career.

And it's about setting the agenda for your market.

You Are Not Your Title

You are your results.

You might be the VP of Marketing.
You might be the Head of Product.
You might be the Founder.

But you're more than the job you're currently in.

Escaping the Existing Market Trap means owning the full weight of your thinking, your belief, your impact—not just your title.

You stop being seen as the executor.
You become the architect.
The creator. The innovator.
The category designer.
The person who didn't just build the product—but reframed the problem.

That's how your career becomes nonlinear.
That's how people start calling you to lead new categories, new companies, new portfolios, new eras.

What's a nonlinear career?
It's the difference between getting promoted …
And getting called in to design what comes next.

What It Changes

When you escape the Existing Market Trap, here's what happens:

> Your company gets clarity.

> But you get credibility.
> Strategic credibility
> Belief-building credibility
> Market-making credibility

You're no longer the one who built a good product.
You're the one who helped the world see a new problem—and built belief.

That's a very different résumé.
That's a very different next chapter.

The Career Multiplier No One Talks About

Escaping the Existing Market Trap gives you leverage—not just in this company, but in every move that comes after.

Because the truth is:

> Category Designers don't get boxed in.
> Category Designers don't get commoditized.
> Category Designers get invited into the room—before the product exists.

They're the people investors want.
The people founders want beside them.
The people the market remembers.

Escaping the Existing Market Trap gives you the story that turns into your next job, your next company, your next raise.

Because in a world where most people work on the incremental, they produce the exponential. They are not trying to improve the past.

They are working to create a different future.

As AI continues to do more and more of the incremental work, people with a track record of exponential become more valuable. And people who view themselves as value creators are turbo-charged with AI.

The time of the AI-powered, one-person, one-billion-dollar company is coming.

Own the Frame. Change the Game.

If you've ever felt:

> Misunderstood
> Mislabeled
> Underestimated
> "I know what this is, but no one else sees it yet"

Then this book isn't just about your company.

It's about you.

Here's the truth. You're known by the company you keep. If your company is creating different futures, you'll be seen as someone with a superpower.

That's why so many people want to work for the Category Kings. If you create or work for a company setting big agendas—building the future shaping things, a company that's changing the world—

The world will see *you* as a world changer.

One big win will create a halo for life.

That's why we think being a category designer is the greatest thing you can be in business.

You don't need permission.
You don't need validation.

You need a strategy.
And you've got it now.

Design the category.
Escape the trap.
Build the career only you could have.

8

What the Existing Market Trap Means for Your Portfolio

The Next Unicorn Isn't Hiding. It's Trapped In The Wrong Category

You meet a sharp founder.
You love the product.
The demo lands.
The TAM slide looks big.
There's an analyst covering the category.
There's customer traction.
There's even a GTM plan.

So you write the check.

And then ... nothing.

Pipeline grows, but deal velocity slows.
Net Promoter Score (NPS) looks okay, but revenue plateaus.
The product gets better, but the story gets weaker.
Sales churn.
Customer confusion.
Team burnout.
And before long, you're looking at a deck that says "Category Creation" for the third quarter in a row—and nobody believes it anymore.

What happened to your investment?

They built a product inside someone else's frame.
They chased demand instead of creating belief.
They didn't change how the market thinks.
They fell into the Existing Market Trap.

And if you're being honest, so did you.

It Doesn't Just Destroy Companies. It Destroys Return Potential.

The Existing Market Trap isn't just a strategy problem.
It's a portfolio drag.

Here's what it does to your fund performance:

> Turns promising companies into perpetual explainers
> Kills top-line growth just when Series B or C conviction is needed
> Deflates exit multiples (because buyers don't understand the strategic value)
> Misses IPO windows (because the company doesn't look like

> a category leader)
> Quietly poisons the internal brand of a firm—because "they can't seem to break out"

The companies you thought would return the fund?

They stall out not because they didn't build something important—but because the market never believed.

You've Seen This Before

You've had a portfolio company with a great product that never got the attention it deserved.

You've sat in board meetings asking:

"Why is growth flat?"
"Why don't analysts cover us?"
"Why can't sales land bigger deals?"
"What's wrong with this story?"

You've pushed them to reposition.
To re-message.
To go upmarket.
To hire a new Chief Marketing Officer (CMO).
To find a new Ideal Customer Profile (ICP).
To just sell harder.

But it doesn't work.

Because the category is still the same.

And they're still not seen as the leader.

The Mistake: Betting on Products Instead of Market Belief

Most investment decisions hinge on product, team, market, and momentum.

But those don't create belief.

Belief comes from:

> Framing a problem the world hasn't named yet
> Claiming the category that solves it
> Creating urgency around it
> Aligning the entire company to lead it

That's what Category Design does.

The longer a company stays in the trap, the harder it is to get out.

The Shift: What the Great Investors Do

The best investors don't (just) look at the product.

They ask:

> What problem does this company really solve?
> Does the market feel that problem?
> What are the economic consequences of the problem?
> What is the category potential?
> Who's framing and naming the category?
> Are we seen as one of many—or the only?
> Is there a clear path to becoming a Category King?

And when they invest, they don't just push for GTM execution.

They push for Category Creation.

They introduce Category Designers.
They pressure-test the POV.
They fund the first Lightning Strike.
They hold the bar for belief—not just Annual Recurring Revenue (ARR).

Because they know:

Category is the multiplier.
When you invest in a company, you're first investing in a category.
If there's no legendary new category, you're not investing in a Category King.

The Risk You're Carrying

Here's the uncomfortable truth:

The Existing Market Trap is probably in your portfolio right now.

You have a company that's stuck in someone else's story.
You have a founder who's explaining instead of evangelizing.
You have a team that's fighting for market share in a market they didn't design.
You have a category that was inherited, not created.

And unless that changes soon, the next round is going to be harder.
The next buyer is going to be less strategic.
The story is going to stay soft.
And you're going to write down a company that could have been great.

Your Move

Here's what you can do—starting today:

> Run an Existing Market Trap Diagnostic across your portfolio
> Spot which companies are trapped
> Introduce this book and language to your founders
> Help them frame the problem—not just pitch the product
> Push for a Point of View (POV)
> Fund a category-defining moment
> Encourage exec alignment around the POV
> Build belief before chasing scale

Category Design isn't a side project.
It's how the best companies pull away.
And it's how the best portfolios outperform.

The Play Bigger POV

The best investments don't chase the biggest TAM.

They create it.
The Existing Market Trap is killing return potential across the board—and the sooner you help your companies escape, the faster they can lead.

> You're not just funding product-market fit.
> You're betting on belief-market fit.
> Make sure they are creating it.

A Cautionary Tale: AI & Categories

*AI Won't Save Your Category.
It's Here To Eat It.*

The Cranes Were Right There

In the late 1970s, the executive team at a time-sharing company called Tymshare met at their Cupertino HQ to talk strategy. The topic: personal computing.

After some debate, the team unanimously agreed personal computing wasn't a threat.

PCs were toys. Tymshare was a real business—enterprise software, terminals, time-sharing.

Through the window of that very conference room, you could see the cranes building Apple's new headquarters.

Tymshare's executives couldn't see the future—even though it was literally right in front of them.

AI Is the New Platform Shift. And Most Companies Are Getting It Wrong.

Here's the caution:

Slapping "AI" onto the end of your pitch doesn't make you an AI category creator.

It just makes you a bolt-on. And everyone can smell it—including investors.

We've seen this movie before:

> When Siebel added "cloud" to its messaging, Salesforce had already designed the SAAS category.
> When Yahoo tried to become social, Facebook had already built a native network.
> When Microsoft stuck a stylus on a laptop, Apple had already turned the phone into a platform.

Every platform shift creates two types of companies:

1. Those that bolt it on
2. Those that design from it

Guess which ones become Category Kings?

Fundamental Shifts Create Category Moments

Every major tech wave gives birth to new categories and a new class of companies:

> Mainframe → Mini → PC → Microsoft, Intel
> Internet → Amazon, Google
> Mobile + Social → Facebook, Uber
> Cloud + SaaS → Salesforce, Snowflake
> Now: Artificial Intelligence

Each transition rewards the companies that are native to the shift—not the ones who simply adapt to it.

AI is not a feature.
AI is a foundation.

And most of today's "AI companies" are bolting it onto last decade's categories.

The Emerging AI Trap

There's a reason this chapter sits inside a book about the Existing Market Trap:

> AI isn't just a breakthrough—it's a trap magnet.
> Why?
> Because 9 out of 10 founders are saying things like:
> "We're the AI-powered version of [legacy category]."
> "It's like Salesforce meets ChatGPT."
> "We're a better copilot for [function]."
> "We added an AI layer to [old SaaS tool]."

> That's not category creation.
> That's category camouflage.
> Investors see it.
> Customers sense it.
> And the market doesn't move.

New Categories Create New Categories

This is the part most people miss.

The biggest breakthroughs in AI won't come from replacing what already exists.
They'll come from revealing problems we didn't even know could be solved.

That's what Category Design does.

AI doesn't just create efficiency.
It unlocks entirely new categories around:

> Autonomous decision systems
> Generative creative infrastructure
> Predictive supply chains
> AI-native collaboration
> Agent economies

The winners won't just build features on top of these ideas.
They'll name the problem.
They'll frame the villain.
They'll build belief.
And they'll design a category the market didn't know it was missing.

Who's Already Doing It?

> Runway didn't build a video editor. They created a new category: AI-powered creative automation.
> Hippocratic isn't a Large Language Model (LLM) for healthcare. It's designing safety-first AI for regulated environments.
> Harvey isn't just building legal chatbots—it's leading a movement around AI-native legal infrastructure.
> Safebooks didn't build an AI financial app—it's solving a problem every company has, but could not solve without AI: financial data governance.

These companies aren't "adding AI" to old categories.
They're building new ones that only AI can enable.

The Numbers Are Wild—and So Is the Trap

As of early 2025:

> There are ~70,000 AI startups worldwide.
> The global AI market is valued at over $390 billion.
> Nvidia has crossed a $3 trillion market cap.
> OpenAI is valued at $157 billion.

And yet ... the vast majority of startups are chasing funding with the same story:

"We're like [old company], but AI."

That's not the future.
That's an AI reswizzle of the past.
That's a feature war dressed up in fancy LLM.

Chasing Today's Problems

Most people chase today's problems (AKA: existing markets).

A powerful way to think about potential new futures is to look at the hot new categories of today and ask:

What category potential could emerge in their wake?

If you're smart (and now's a dumb time to be dumb), you'll unshackle yourself from the present.
You'll engage with future-focused people.
You'll ask weird questions.
And you'll start playing with the next growth opportunities.

Play this game:

Given that this is true now, what might that mean for new categories and adjacent ones?

You buy a nice car → You need a car cover.
You buy a smartphone → Now you need a case. Or financing. Or a smartwatch.

The solution creates demand.
The demand creates the aisle.

Today's Solutions Are Tomorrow's Problems

Every new solution creates new problems:

> You buy tools to care for your house → Now you need a place to store them

> Nvidia chips get deployed at scale → Now we need more data centers, more energy, more cooling
> AI agents take action → Now we need trust layers, coordination systems, monitoring infrastructure
> Native digital kids grow up → We need digital parenting tools, time trackers, safety blockers

If you want to build the markets of tomorrow, ask:

What problems will today's solutions create?

Jam on that with the smartest, most curious, most future-attached people you know.

That's where the real categories are hiding.

The Opportunity—and the Warning

AI is the biggest wave since the Internet, arguably ever.

And like every wave before it, it will create new categories, trap legacy players, reward native thinkers and punish the bolt-ons.

Don't add AI to your pitch deck.
Design your category from it.

If you're a founder building in AI, ask yourself:

> What new problem does AI make visible?
> What villain is only now possible to fight?
> What hero is being born in this new world?
> What category needs to exist—but hasn't been named yet?

That's where the power is.

Play Bigger POV

You don't build a movement by updating your messaging.
You build it by designing the category AI makes possible.
If you're adding AI to last decade's pitch deck, you're Tymshare.
And if you listen closely …
You can hear the cranes outside your window.

Appendices

Appendix A

For the Founders Who Took the Shot

A dedication—and a quiet truth.
The people mentioned in this book are founders and CEOs who have worked their asses off to put a dent in the universe.

They've built real companies.
Led real teams.
Shipped real products.
Some created legendary categories. Others didn't.

That's kind of the point—not everyone wins the category war.

But every founder in this book took the shot.

And we want to be clear about something up front:

Just because a company didn't win the category doesn't mean the founder failed.

Our co-author, Al Ramadan, learned that the hard way.

He spent seven years at Quokka Sports, working to change the way people experienced live sports—pioneering what he called Total Sports Immersion.

They helped create the digital sports media category before it had a name.
They went public on NASDAQ at a billion-dollar valuation.

Three years later, the company shut down.

Was it a failure? In some ways, yes.
But twenty-five years later, the way we experience sport has completely changed—and the vision Quokka had is now the default.

Co-author Christopher Lochhead was the founding CMO of Internet consulting juggernaut, Scient. In three years (by Q1 2000) the firm became the category king, with over 1,000 people and was a public company with a $9 billion market cap. When the dot-com bubble burst it took Scient with it.

The company helped build some of the earliest, most successful Internet businesses. Then, poof!

Was it a failure? Yes.
But twenty-five years later, was it worth it? Yes. Creating a different future, shooting for the exponential, always is. And they helped (a little) pioneer the commercial Internet.

There are so many factors that determine success:
Timing. Capital. People. Partners. The stock market. The weather.

Some of those are in your control. Some aren't.

What's in your control is what you believe.

What you build.
What you leave on the field.

And here's what we know about the founders and CEOs in this book:

They're courageous.
They're committed.
And they're giving it everything they've got.

This book is for them.
And because of them.

A Quick Note on the Stories You Don't See
In writing this book, we poured over a decade's worth of powerful learning from working alongside extraordinary founders.

Many of those insights made the cut.

But plenty—often the best and juiciest—didn't.

The truth is, the most impactful lessons usually come from the moments where things went sideways. But sharing those openly involves navigating legal landmines we simply couldn't overcome.

So, if you ever feel like buying us a round (or seven), we'll gladly share some off-the-record tales and hard-earned wisdom left on the cutting room floor—stories just a bit too colorful, honest, or risky for print.

Because sometimes, the best lessons are best shared over drinks—not pages.

Appendix B

The 13 Deadly Sins Taxonomy

The Existing Market Trap Taxonomy

If you study any Category King, you'll find this pattern: they don't just sell a product—they teach the world how to think. They name the problem, define the solution, and build a taxonomy that organizes the chaos their customers feel.

A taxonomy, coupled with new languaging[3]—the strategic use of words to change thinking—is how leaders educate the market. It's how they frame the game they're playing—and why it's different from everything that came before.

And how they drive word-of-mouth. WOM is, was, and always has been the greatest way to build belief.

So we built our own taxonomy.

These 13 Deadly Sins are the problem clusters we've seen across hundreds of startups and scale-ups.

---

[3] https://www.categorypirates.news/p/category-design-tip-use-languaging?utm_source=publication-search/.

They are the symptoms of the Existing Market Trap—the invisible forces that cause great products, teams, and companies to stall and fail.

Some sins appear early. Others show up just before the fall.

But they all come from the same root problem: failing to design the market you want to win by building belief in a new solution.

Use this list as a diagnostic tool.

A lens for self-evaluation.

Use it to challenge your own assumptions.
And most of all—use it to escape the trap before it's too late.

#1 – The Engineer's Dilemma
You fall in love with the product and forget to design the market.

#2 – The Obviously Better Fallacy
You assume being faster, cheaper, or more advanced will be enough to win—without changing the frame of the game.

#3 – The Pinball Effect
You bounce from feedback to feature with no point of view, no North Star, and no strategy to escape the noise.

#4 – The Horizontal Tool Illusion
You build something flexible for everyone—and end up resonating with no one.

#5 – The Product-Led Growth Myth
You rely on self-serve growth loops to carry the company, but hit a wall because even legendary products can't speak for themselves.

#6 – The Market Share Fantasy

You chase a slice of a giant TAM instead of designing a new market you can actually lead.

#7 – The Sales Hype Machine

You hire sellers to "go faster" before you've nailed the POV, leading to confusion, struggle, churn, and pipeline fiction.

#8 – The Distribution Delusion

You mistake reach for power, thinking that access to customers is the same as owning a category.

#9 – The VC Pressure Cooker

You raise big, grow fast, and sacrifice clarity for speed—only to find yourself trapped inside a market you didn't design.

#10 – The Conglomerate Identity Crisis

You have too many products for too many buyers and end up with no clear POV, no obvious enemy, no obvious hero, and no lane to lead.

#11 – The Brand Vanity Obsession

You polish the logo, tune the tagline, and obsess over brand perception—without fixing the real problem—how are you going to design and dominate a giant new category that matters?

#12 – The Point Tool Ceiling

You solve one piece of the problem, get pigeonholed as a feature, and stall out before reaching platform scale.

#13 – The Existential Decline

You are still the Category King—but the market (problem definition) has moved beyond that category, and you haven't.

Appendix C

This Is Where The Real Work Begins

How to Use This Primer: Inside your company. Inside yourself.

This book isn't a strategy deck.

It's a tool.

Use it with your exec team.

Bring it into your offsite.

Use the chapters as diagnostics.

Run a "Which Sin Are We In?" session with your board.

Start the conversation nobody wants to have—but everybody feels.

You don't need permission.

You don't need a consultant.

You just need the courage to name the problem.

The Existing Market Trap Diagnostic

What Sin Are You In?

The fastest way to escape the trap is to name it.

That's why we built the Existing Market Trap Diagnostic[4]—a short, punch-you-in-the-face tool to help founders, CEOs, and operators figure out which of the 13 sins they're stuck in.

You'll answer 6 questions.

We'll show you the top 3 deadly sins you're in—and what to do about it.

It's fast. It's sharp.
It's designed for people building companies in real time.

How to Get Your Exec Team Aligned on the Shift

Category Design isn't something the CEO decides and announces. It's a shift in how the entire company thinks, builds, and communicates.

Here's how to get the team aligned:
- Share the Primer – Ask each exec to read Chapters 1, 3, 4, and 5
- Run a POV Debrief – What's our current story? Who believes it? Who doesn't?
- Start with the Problem – Ask, "*What is the problem we're really solving?*" Then ask, "*Do our customers feel it?*"
- Use the Diagnostic[5] – Do it together. Score yourselves. Make it safe to say, "we're stuck."
- Don't start with naming the category – Start with naming the pain. The rest flows from there.

---

4   https://playbigger.com/EMTDiagnostic/.
5   Same as link 4 – Ibid.

- Host a half-day offsite – Use the 10 POV elements as a framework. Build the first draft together.
- Expect tension – If there's no argument, you're not there yet.

Category Design only works when belief is shared.
You can't align the company until you align the room.

How to Sell the Change Upstream (Board & Investors)

You'll need to bring your investors along. Here's how to do it:
- Reframe the problem – Use Chapter 1. Show the cost of staying stuck in the wrong category.
- Show the strategic ceiling – Explain why GTM, pricing, and product expansion have hit a wall.
- Use the Diagnostic[6] – Share your Deadly Sin score. Make it real.
- Present the new POV as a growth driver, not a pivot – This is about going bigger, not changing direction.
- Ask for their help – Investors want leverage. Category Design is the lever.
- Position the Lightning Strike as a board-level event – Make them part of the moment. Invite them in.

Most investors want you to "break out"—they just don't always know what's holding you back.

Show them the trap.
Then show them the way out.

---

6   Same as link 4 – Ibid.

The *Deadly Sin Drop* Series

Follow the next chapters as they're written.

We're not holding the rest of the book behind a wall.

We're releasing the remaining sin chapters in public—one every two weeks—through the *Existing Market Trap Deadly Sin Drop Series*.

Each drop includes:
- A full Deadly Sin chapter
- Real founder insight
- A field guide you can use in your company, boardroom, or next GTM offsite
- A direct CTA to escape

You can read them in real time.
You can send them to your team.
You can share your sin—and help shape the next chapter.

- Subscribe to the Deadly Sin Drop Series[7]
- Submit your story[8]

One Last Reminder

Most people stay trapped.
Most companies die slowly—buried in someone else's market.
Most founders never get credit for what they really built.

You don't have to be **most**.

---

[7] Subscribe here: https://www.playbigger.com/newsletter.
[8] Submit your story here: https://playbigger.com/EMTStory/.

> Design the category.
> Escape the trap.
> Let's go.

When in doubt, email Mary Grice: mary@playbigger.com

Appendix D

One More Thing—We Need to Talk About Positioning

The Trap Hiding in Plain Sight

There's a tradition we started in *Play Bigger*.

We save one last thing for the end. Not because it's an afterthought—but because it changes how you see everything that came before.

In *Play Bigger*, we needed a foil. So we picked SAP.

Not to be petty—but because SAP had become the poster child for old-school strategy.
They were the system. And we wanted to challenge it.

But in this book, we're not going after SAP.
We're going after something bigger. Something more dangerous.

> We're going after a belief.

It's a belief that's been repeated so many times—by founders, VCs, accelerators, analysts, and agencies—that no one even questions it anymore.

> It's called **Positioning.**

And what we're going to say about it might piss some people off. That's okay. Because this conversation is long overdue.

The Truth About Positioning

On the surface, positioning seems harmless.
Even smart. Strategic. Responsible.

"We need a better positioning statement."
"Let's reposition our product."
"We should hire a positioning firm."

But let's call it what it really is:

A trap.

Because positioning—by definition—is about placing your company inside an existing market.
It assumes the aisle already exists. The category already has a name. And your job is to fit.

You're not changing the game.

You're learning how to play it—slightly better, slightly faster, slightly louder than the next guy.

You're jockeying for attention in a market someone else already leads.

What Positioning Used to Be

When Al Ries and Jack Trout published *Positioning: The Battle for Your Mind* in 1981, their idea was radical:

Own a single idea in the customer's brain.

Volvo = Safety
Coca-Cola = Americana
BMW = Driving

Genius.

But over time, positioning lost its soul.

It stopped being about focus.
It became a messaging tweak. A spreadsheet exercise. A rebrand.
It stopped being about owning a category—and became about surviving inside one.

Today's Positioning Is the Status Quo in Disguise
Here's what most people mean when they say "positioning" today:

"We found a big market."
"We built something better."
"Now let's position it against the competition."

It sounds smart—until you realize what you're fighting for:

The 24%.

Because that's what's left after the Category King takes their cut.

Category Kings earn 76% of the market cap.

Everyone else fights over what's left.

So when you position your way into a hot market—without naming the game, without defining the problem, without designing the category—you're not building a legendary company.

You're just signing up to be a sidekick in someone else's story. (And probably a losing one.)

Compared to What?

Some will tell you:

"Category Design is too hard. Too bold. Too expensive."

They'll say:

Why not just reposition?
Add some AI.
Reframe the tagline.
That's faster.

To which we say: Compared to what?

Compared to:
- Building something legendary?
- Creating a new frame of value?
- Leading a market that didn't exist before?

If that's the goal—
Why would you not name it?
Why would you not lead it?

Why would you settle for squeezing into a Gartner quadrant ...
... when you could create your own axis?

365,000 People Fighting for the 24%

Go search "positioning" on LinkedIn.

Click "People."

You'll find over 365,000 professionals with "positioning" in their title or bio.

That's a whole army of smart, talented humans ...
All trying to out-message each other in a market they didn't invent.

Webinars. Copywriting. Competitive grids.
Everyone is trying to move one square to the left in an Industry Analyst's market map.

Meanwhile, the Category Kings?
They're building a new board.

It Would Be Awesome—If It Were True
Positioning says:

Find a big market.
Build a better mousetrap.
Position your better mousetrap clearly.
The world will beat a path to your door.

It would be awesome.
If it were true.

But it's not.

It's a trap.

You Don't Need a Better Position. You Need a Better Frame.
If you're reading this, you're probably not trying to get second—or fifth—place.

You're not trying to rank higher in a market someone else defined.

You're trying to build something legendary.

So here's the truth:

Positioning puts you in a market.
Category Design puts you in the lead.

Positioning asks, *"Where do we fit?"*
Category Design asks, *"What kind of future are we building?"*

One keeps you trapped.
The other sets you free.

Choose wisely, young Jedi.

Appendix E

Methodology Behind the $17 Trillion Estimate

To understand the scale of global innovation investment—and the scale of its failure—we took a comprehensive view of capital flows into startups, scaleups, and breakthrough technologies over the past decade (2014–2024).

What's Included in the $17 Trillion

The headline figure (~$17 Trillion) reflects actual deployed capital, not just dry powder or fundraising commitments. It includes:

- **Venture Capital** (all stages, globally)
- **Private Equity** focused on tech-enabled and innovation-driven firms (growth equity, minority, and buyouts)
- **Corporate Venture Capital** investments from strategic arms of large enterprises
- **Angel & Seed funding** (including syndicates, micro-funds, and early-stage platforms)
- **Family Office and Sovereign Wealth Fund** allocations to private tech deals
- **Accelerator & incubator** equity programs
- **Venture debt and structured credit** earmarked for startups and scaleups

Our data sources include PitchBook, Crunchbase, Bain & Company, McKinsey, CB Insights, and public equity market data (via Bloomberg, Nasdaq).

Startup Failure Rates and Capital Erosion

The claim that ~90% of funded companies failed to deliver a return is grounded in multiple industry-wide studies. This includes companies that shut down, stagnated, or exited at valuations below their invested capital.

Of the estimated 180,000 companies that received funding during this period, only a fraction achieved exits that returned capital to investors—let alone outperformed.

This results in a staggering $13 Trillion in unrealized or impaired capital, including:

- Write-offs from failed or zombie startups
- Devalued unicorns with no clear exit path
- Unsold private equity holdings accumulating in LP portfolios
- Late-stage markdowns in 2022–2024 as the ZIRP era ended

In 2024 alone, more than $2 trillion in value was erased, driven by a public tech correction and its knock-on effects in the private markets.

Sources Consulted

1. **PitchBook–NVCA Venture Monitor**, Q4 2024; deal-value tables (2014–2024).
2. **Bain & Co.**, Global Private Equity Report series (2014–2025); buyout and growth-equity deal values.
3. **McKinsey & Co.**, Global Private Markets Review 2024,

Exhibits 1 & 2.

4. **PitchBook** platform extract, "VC-backed companies" dataset (snapshot as of May 17, 2025).

5. **ExplodingTopics**, "Startup Failure Statistics 2025"; Embroker, "106 Startup Statistics for 2024".

6. **Bain & Co.**, "Record $3.2 Trillion in Unsold PE Assets" (Chief Investment Officer report, Feb 2024).

7. **Axios Pro**, "Aging U.S. Unicorns Now Worth $2.5 Trillion" (Nov 2024).

8. **Bloomberg**, "Nasdaq-100 Plunges into Correction, Wiping $2 Trillion+" (Aug 2, 2024).

About the Authors

Al Ramadan is the co-founder and CEO of Play Bigger, LLC, and co-author of *Play Bigger,* the book that launched Category Design into the world. A Fortran programmer and mathematician turned tech executive, Al took Quokka Sports public during the first wave of digital media and later helped lead Macromedia through its rise and acquisition by Adobe, where he served on the executive team. He's spent decades helping founders build legendary companies by designing new markets—creating more than $50 billion in market cap along the way. Equal parts strategist, storyteller, and surf junkie, Al is known for bringing out the best in people and pushing teams to see what's possible—then making it real.

Christopher Lochhead is a "Godfather of Category Design" and 14-time #1 bestselling co-author. Best known for *Play Bigger, Snow Leopard, Creator Capitalist* & *22 Laws of Category Design*. He's host of podcast Follow Your Different, has advised over 50 VC-backed startups, was CMO of three public tech companies and is co-founder of Category Pirates and Play Bigger Advisors. The Marketing Journal named him "one of the best minds in marketing" and The Economist calls him, "off-putting to some."

Jason Wellcome is a partner at Play Bigger, LLC. where he advises founders, CEOs, and Fortune 500s on category design and market creation. A longtime strategist and former agency leader, he's helped shape the narratives and go-to-market strategies behind some of the tech industry's most iconic companies—from breakout start-ups to global giants like Cloudflare, Docusign and Microsoft.

Mary Grice, a rare Silicon Valley native, has been with Play Bigger LLC since day one. Now as a Partner and the Chief Operating Officer. Mary is responsible for execution, building relationships with CEOs, Founders and Investors interested in creating and dominating new markets and is integral to every client engagement. And in her other life, she runs an urban fruit orchard with her partner in crime (sister) Kari.

Made in the USA
Columbia, SC
02 June 2025

47903eb3-d8b9-4126-9abc-d8cadc519371R01